Potters Use Clay

Carter Hayn

Rosen REAL READERS

Rosen Classroom™
New York

Clay comes from the earth.
It is soft when wet.
It is hard when dry.

A potter makes
things with clay.
This potter is going
to make a vase.

He puts clay on a potter's wheel.
The wheel spins.
It is used to make things round.

The potter shapes the clay.
Clay is easy to shape
when it is wet.

The potter pushes
the clay down.
He is shaping the bottom
of the vase.

The potter pulls the clay up
on the sides.
He shapes the clay
into a vase.

The potter puts the vase in a kiln.

A kiln is a kind of oven.

It is used to make clay hard.

The temperature in the kiln rises to more than 800 degrees. The vase bakes for many hours.

The potter takes the vase
out of the kiln.
It is now hard.

The vase cools off.

It is now safe to touch.

The potter paints the vase.

Words to Know

clay

kiln

potter's wheel

vase